KENNETH'S FIRST PLAY

Richard Nelson
&
Colin Chambers

BROADWAY PLAY PUBLISHING INC
New York
www.broadwayplaypublishing.com
info@broadwayplaypublishing.com

KENNETH'S FIRST PLAY

Cover photo compliments of The Royal Shakespeare Company

First edition: September 2004
This edition: October 2017
I S B N: 978-0-88145-232-7

Book design: Marie Donovan
Word processing: Microsoft Word for Windows
Typographic controls: Xerox Ventura Publisher 2.0 P E
Typeface: Palatino

CONTENTS

INTRODUCTION

KENNETH'S FIRST PLAY is an attempt to explore the world of plays by taking the audience on an unexpected theatrical journey. We follow the adventures of Kenneth as he makes his first trip to a theater, which doesn't turn out to be quite what he anticipated. Bored by what he sees on stage, he tries to leave but goes through the wrong door and finds himself lost inside the play.

After performances of KENNETH'S FIRST PLAY, in discussions with the audience, we were invariably asked "Why did you write it?" The answer we gave always began with the fact that we were both parents. Although we came from different countries—one from America and one from England—we both had similar experiences of taking our children to the theater and longing for something to go and see with them that bridged the gap between the worlds of children's and adult theater.

We decided we would try to write such a piece. We approached the task as two people with skills in the professional theater rather than as specialists in education. Our desire was to use our experience to open a door into the world of plays, and the key, we believed, was the imagination. We wanted to release the power of the imagination in the way that only theater can. We wanted to write a play that would ask such questions as "what is a play?", "why do we tell stories about our lives in play form?", "why have we

done so for more than two thousand years?" We
wanted KENNETH'S FIRST PLAY to be challenging
but we also wanted it to be fun.

We always intended the play to have a wide use,
and have made suggestions in the Commentary and
Notes at the back of the book on methods of doing this.
We offer staging variations —for example, changes that
allow the central role to be female and vocabulary
adjustments for North America—and curriculum ideas.
These are divided into issues and themes, topics for
class and/or homework, and ways of using the play
in lesson plans or schemes of work related to various
age groups (linked to their Key Stages in the British
National Curriculum systems and approximate grades
in U S schools).

The play, which lasts approximately forty-five
minutes, was first presented by a professional theater
company, and, in the way the performances were
programmed, it was possible for the play to be seen
both by families and by school parties, including people
who were going on to see a full-length show. It was also
possible to take in a tour of the theater as well.

We tested our ideas with this company, the Royal
Shakespeare Company, and developed the text through
two internal workshops. A first version was given a
week-long workshop in the R S C's small theater, The
Other Place, in Stratford-upon-Avon. Six actors in the
company (Martina Laird, Emma Poole, Philip Quast,
Adrian Schiller, Alisdair Simpson, Jacqueline York)
under the direction of Michael Attenborough rehearsed
a script that we revised as the week unfolded. At the
end of the workshop, we rewrote the script more
substantially.

This new text, now called KENNETH'S FIRST PLAY,
was subsequently performed after a week's rehearsal in
the R S C's Pit theater in London (with David Tennant
replacing Philip Quast). There were three shows for

invited school's audiences, who were asked to act as guinea pigs and give us their reactions.

The schools that came were all from neighboring London boroughs: Central Foundation, Cumberland, Hampstead, Islington Green, Highbury Fields, Highbury Grove, Langdon Park, Mount Carmel, Sir John Cass. They covered an age range from 9/10 to 15/16, and there were also students aged 16/17 from Beacon Lodge College in Sussex.

Responses came in small and whole group discussion immediately after each show and some schools sent us class and homework that had been produced later as a follow-up to the visit. Generally, the children liked the opening moments, when Kenneth sits among the audience talking out loud about how bored he is, the *Romeo and Juliet* scene, and the scene in Kenneth's home when he pretends to be his mother.

We digested all this feedback, plus comments from the few adults whom we had asked to attend, and rewrote once more. Three months later, with a new group of actors (whose names are listed at the front of the book), KENNETH'S FIRST PLAY was given its public premiere at the Swan Theatre in Stratford-upon-Avon and was subsequently to tour to Newcastle, Plymouth and London.

KENNETH'S FIRST PLAY premiered at the Swan
Theatre, Stratford-upon-Avon, on 18 June 1997.
The cast was as follows:

KENNETH . . . . John Killoran
ACTOR 1 . . . . .Paul Jesson
ACTOR 2 . . . . .Nadine Marshall
ACTOR 3 . . . . .Shuna Snow
ACTOR 4 . . . . Barry Aird
ACTOR 5 . . . . Victoria Pritchard

Directors . . . . Richard Nelson and Colin Chambers
Stage Manage . . . . Eric Lumsden
Lighting Designer . . . . Wayne Dowdeswell

Thanks to John Woolf for help with the music.

Our thanks to Maria Evans, Jocelyn Nelson,
Zoe Nelson, Adrian Noble and Jane Noble.

to Zoe and Jocelyn
to Beth and Ben

(Scene: Induction)

(A bare stage, except for a rehearsal door/doorframe, stage center, and two benches. [One should be long enough to seat five actors.] One bench is to the left, one to the right— the "wings" from which the actors, when not "on stage", watch the show, perform music effects and sound cues.)

(Once the audience is seated, one last audience member arrives, KENNETH. *He is young and innocent.)*

*(*KENNETH *looks around and, thinking he sees an empty space, starts to press his way past others. He carries a bag of crisps and a can of Coke.)*

*(*KENNETH *is all smiles; he has never been to a play before.)*

(As he pushes his way along:)

KENNETH: Excuse me. Pardon me. Boy, am I excited. Nice shirt. Is there a seat there? *(He points to the middle of a row—but there is no room there. As he makes his way:)* Sorry, was that a foot? *(Holding up his crisps)* They're selling 'em in the foyer! *(Reaching the middle)* Mind if I just—. Squeeze over a little. Come on! Squeeze. Thank you.

(He starts to sit, then immediately stands to take off his coat. He hands his crisps and Coke to a child in the audience to hold for him.)

KENNETH: Would you be so kind? *(Taking off his coat)* So—this is a play! Is this going to be great? My first play. *(He folds his coat and sits on it. Turns around.)* I'm not blocking anyone, am I? *(He is. Shaking hands)* Kenneth.

(The actor playing KENNETH *can improvise with the audience.)*

(He sits, triumphant, very pleased with himself. He offers crisps to his neighbours and asks:)

KENNETH: Did I miss anything? I hope not. *(Pause. Suddenly yawns and is bored)* When's it going to start? Really nice shirt. Comfortable? *(He opens a can of Coke; perhaps some Coke spurts across the stage. Oblivious to the mess, he sits, eager, in happy anticipation.)*

(The ACTORS, *two men and three women, enter in a line, humming a Greek chant. They line up across the stage with their backs to the audience, giving their version of a Greek Chorus.)*

*(*ACTOR 1, *center stage, turns and addresses the audience, in the deep voice of a scholar:)*

ACTOR 1: The play, historically, began two thousand years ago with the ancient Greeks.

*(*KENNETH, *smiling, looks around to see if his neighbors are enjoying themselves.)*

(The "Chorus" reaches a quick climax of humming/moaning and dramatically stops, as suddenly ACTOR 4 *turns, making a loud musical sound [e.g. banging a drum, clashing cymbals, blowing a trumpet]. This startles* KENNETH *who throws his crisps [potato chips] up in the air.)*

*(*ACTOR 2 *turns.)*

ACTOR 2: The play, many people believe, only came into its own four hundred years ago with the genius of William Shakespeare.

*(*ACTOR 5 *begins to make a melancholy sound [e.g. on a recorder, a guitar, a balalaika].* ACTOR 3 *turns.)*

ACTOR 3: The play—as we know it today—it can be argued—derives from the Russian playwright, Anton Chekhov, who lived a mere one hundred years ago.

KENNETH: *(To others in the audience)* The play began, when? *(Holds up his watch.)* About a minute ago if you ask me! *(He laughs at his joke.)*

(The STAGE MANAGER has hurried down the aisle and points to KENNETH and "shs" him, then returns back to his place. KENNETH listens again.)

ACTOR 3: *(Steps forward, continuing)* Anton Chekhov is probably a name you are not familiar with.

KENNETH: *(Eating)* Am I the only one bored already? *(Laughs)*

ACTOR 3: What is important to know is that in the plays he wrote—

(KENNETH makes a huge, dramatic yawn to show he is bored.)

ACTOR 3: —his characters did not speak in poetry.

ACTOR 2: *(Steps forward)* As Shakespeare's characters do.

ACTOR 1: *(Steps forward)* And those of the ancient Greeks.

ACTOR 3: They spoke—

KENNETH: This is soooo boring!!

ACTOR 5: *(Steps forward)* Like you and I speak.

ACTOR 4: *(Steps forward, over this)* —in the language of everyday life.

KENNETH: Who cares? I'm getting a headache. What is this—school?

ACTOR 3: *(Trying to ignore KENNETH)* Sometimes his characters would even stop and say....

ALL ACTORS: *(Whispering in unison)* Nothing—.

ACTOR 3: —creating *(Pause)* pauses...

(KENNETH pretends to snore.)

ACTOR 3: ...silences *(Beat)* ...just like we have in real life.

KENNETH: Not in my life! *(He suddenly stands, covers his ears, and makes his way to the stage.)* I can't take this! I've got to get out of here. Where's the exit? Where's the exit? *(He sees the door center stage and heads for that.)* There's the exit! Excuse me. Sorry. What a waste of time.

(The ACTORS panic when they see where he is headed and cry out to warn him:)

ACTORS: Not there! Don't go in there! That's not an exit! Stop!

(KENNETH ignores their warnings and holds them off:)

KENNETH: Get away from me! Get away! I'm going home!

(And he is through the door. The door slams.)

(Scene: In the Play)

ACTOR 4: *(To himself)* Oh my God.

(The ACTORS return to their benches immediately. There is a loud thunderclap made by the STAGE MANAGER offstage.)

(Suddenly the door opens again and KENNETH is apparently thrown by some force onto the stage, as if to the other side of the door he just went through. The door closes behind him. He falls and gasps for breath.)

(The ACTORS make cell noises—dripping water, creaking wood, howling, distant wind.)

KENNETH: *(Anxious)* Is this the foyer? It doesn't look like the foyer. Where am I? *(He hesitates, looks around, stands and goes to the door, and "tries" it. It doesn't open. He bangs three times quickly. To himself)* It's locked.

(ACTOR 1 approaches KENNETH, who jumps when he sees him. Cell noises stop.)

KENNETH: Who are you? Where did you come from? Why is the door locked?

ACTOR 1: You were trying to leave? But, Kenneth, the show had only just begun.

KENNETH: Where am I? *(Suddenly suspicious.)* Kenneth? How did you know my—name? Look, I didn't do anything. I didn't touch anything! Uh—Is this the foyer? I was coming back.

ACTOR 1: Kenneth...

KENNETH: I had to go to the toilet...!

ACTOR 1: We tried to warn you, but...

KENNETH: But—what? What is this place, anyway?

ACTOR 1: *(To* ACTOR 5, *who, unseen by* KENNETH, *is now behind him.)* Tell him.

ACTOR 5: You're—in the play.

KENNETH: I'm—? Really?? *(Thinks he has figured it out.)* Oh, I get it. I'm...That's the door to... And you're actors. I must have just wandered through the wrong.... I'll be going now. Sorry to... *(He starts to go to the door, stops and looks around.)* So this must be where they make the scenery. Where they do the lights.

ACTOR 5: No, Kenneth. Not backstage. You're not backstage in a theater. You're in the play.

(Beat)

*(*ACTORS *1 and 5 exit through the door—for them it isn't locked—and sit on the benches.* KENNETH *hurries to the door, but it is locked for him. He bangs three times, a little slower.)*

KENNETH: *(Through the door)* I don't understand. What are you talking about?

ACTOR 3: *(Startling him from behind)* Kenneth... Look— you have an audience.

(She shows him the audience.)

(Scene: Romeo and Juliet)

ACTOR 3: *(Gesturing to the audience)* Tell them something. Something you think might interest them. *(Beat)* They're waiting. Good luck.

(She too goes out through the door; KENNETH tries it again. It is still locked for him. He bangs three times, very slowly.)

(KENNETH is alone on stage. He feels self-conscious; he doesn't know what to say. Smiles, looks around, whistles.)

KENNETH: My first play. First—play I've ever been to. Hasn't been—quite what I expected. *(Then suddenly fearing the worst)* But I'm not complaining. *(To whomever might be listening:)* And I wasn't leaving! *(Short pause)* So. This is...a play. Huh. *(Beat)* I only came today because my sister—she's fourteen—she was telling me what a great time she had—at a play. *(Beat)* It's where she met this boy. This boy...who's now her...boyfriend? George. The name of this—boy, that she met at—I think she said "at"—I don't think she said "in" a play. *(Beat)* She went with a school group. A lot of her friends. She said she never had such a good time. So—she'd taken her—

(Door opens as ACTOR 3 enters carrying a chair. The door closes behind her.)

KENNETH: —taken her seat.

(She sets a chair down next to Kenneth, and exits.)

KENNETH: She, er, he, er... This is hard. How do I explain this? She said, he—. Uh. Look, pretend for a minute that I'm my sister. Ruth. *(He sits.)* She—. *(Then he realizes how funny it is.)* Hey. I'm a fourteen-year-old girl. *(Laughs. Then he suddenly does a gross imitation of a fourteen year old girl, pretends to look at herself in the mirror, pulls down her short skirt, looks around self-consciously, then he laughs at his joke.)* And just before the lights go down and the play begins, Ruth sees, I see, sitting next to—me—George.

(ACTOR 2 suddenly steps forward.)

ACTOR 2: I'll play George.

KENNETH: But you're a girl—

ACTOR 2: So what? *(She sits up straight, then asks:)* How old is George?

KENNETH: Fourteen.

ACTOR 2: Oh.

(Then she slouches grotesquely and does her funny imitation of a boy. When she finishes, she turns back to KENNETH and smiles, satisfied.)

KENNETH: *(Introducing ACTOR 2 to the audience)* George. And there was something about her—him—about the way he looked, his smile—

("George" smiles.)

KENNETH: —his eyes, that made my sister—me—well the word she used was—"melt". And the play began.

(Music [e.g. recorder played by another actor] as ACTOR 5 stands.)

KENNETH: I forgot, Ruth forgot, what the play was called.

ACTOR 5: *Romeo and Juliet* by William Shakespeare.

ACTOR 4: *(Stands)* The story of two young people who fall in love.

(ACTORS 4 and 5—one male, one female—begin to perform an extract from Romeo and Juliet *[Act 1, Scene v] behind* KENNETH *and* ACTOR 2.

ACTOR 4: *(Romeo)*
If I profane with my unworthiest hand
This holy shrine, the gentle sin is this.

KENNETH: *(As his sister)* But all I could see before me,
on that stage—was his face. This boy, whose name I
didn't know, sitting next to me.

(KENNETH *turns to catch a glimpse of "George's" face.*)

ACTOR 4: *(Romeo)*
My lips, two blushing pilgrims, ready stand
To smooth that rough touch with a tender kiss.

KENNETH: Something in the play caught my attention.

ACTOR 5: *(Juliet)*
Good pilgrim, you do wrong your hand too much,
Which mannerly devotion shows in this;
For saints have hands that pilgrims' hands do touch,
And palm to palm is holy palmer's kiss.

ACTOR 2: *(As George, looking at* KENNETH)
She's—gorgeous.

ACTOR 4: *(Romeo)*
Have not saints lips, and holy palmers too?

ACTOR 5: *(Juliet)*
Ay, pilgrim, lips that they must use in prayer.

ACTOR 4: *(Romeo)*
I think you're wonderful!

KENNETH & ACTOR 2: *(To audience)* Did he say that!?

KENNETH: *(Whispers to "George")* My name is Ruth.

ACTOR 2: *(Whispers to* KENNETH) And my name's
George.

ACTOR 4: *(Romeo)*
Then move not while my prayer's effect I take.

(Romeo and Juliet kiss.)

(KENNETH *and* ACTOR 2 *look at this kiss, then at each other.*
They feel awkward but are drawn to each other. "George"
stretches, and puts an arm around "Ruth".)

ACTOR 4: *(Romeo)*
Thus from my lips, by thine, my sin is purged.

ACTOR 5: *(Juliet)*
Then have my lips the sin that they have took.

ACTOR 4: *(Romeo)*
Sin from my lips? O trespass sweetly urged! Give me
my sin again.

(They kiss again. Music stops. ACTOR 2 *takes her chair off,*
KENNETH *stands and* ACTOR 5 *takes* KENNETH's *chair off,*
as KENNETH *speaks:)*

KENNETH: And suddenly the lights are on again, people
are applauding and it's over. Where had the time gone?
And where—*(Looks around)* was George?!! *(He runs to*
the door and opens it—it is unlocked.) I run to the foyer.

(He goes out and comes right back in. The other ACTORS *now*
stand and talk among themselves, pretending this is the foyer.
We overhear some of their conversation:)

ACTORS: *(Severally)* What I don't get is why the
characters have to go on and on and on. I mean, we get
it already. He loves her. Why doesn't he just say that?
It's all that—poetry. I agree. No one talks like that.
I think we're meant to know not only what Romeo and
Juliet think but also to feel it. That's what poetry does.
It allows us to feel what they are feeling.

(KENNETH suddenly sees "George" across the foyer.)

KENNETH: There he is. Look at me. Look at me.
(To the audience.) I don't say this. I think this.

("George" turns and looks at KENNETH.*)*

ACTOR 2: *(As George)* There she is. God, why am I so shy?! Why can't I just go up to her and...? *(To the audience)* And what? Is she still looking at me? Is she?

KENNETH: I pretend I need a drink of water. He's near the drinking fountain. *(He goes through the foyer crowd.)* Excuse me. Pardon me.
I almost walk right into him.

(They are face to face. "George" suddenly drops to his knee and unties his shoe.)

ACTOR 2: *(To the audience)* I pretend my shoe is untied.

KENNETH: So do I. *(He drops to his knee.)* Except my shoes don't have any laces.

(He looks at his "shoes", "George" notices, and they both laugh. This breaks the ice.)

KENNETH & ACTOR 2: *(Together)* I love his/her laugh. I think this. *(Beat)* And that smile. *(Beat)* And those lips. I could kiss those lips. *(They stare into each other's eyes, then:)* But instead, I say—"Hi, what school do you come from? Really? That's so close to mine!" *(To audience)* I'm in love. *(They do a "high five".)*

ACTOR 2: Good play, Kenneth!

(The ACTORS, including ACTOR 2, begin to applaud and whistle. This confuses KENNETH.)

ATORS: I loved that play! Terrific! I liked it when we were hearing Romeo and Juliet and your sister and George were falling for each other. They didn't have to say anything. My favorite part. Good play! Good play! —Etc

(They pat KENNETH on the back, shake his hand.)

KENNETH: Wait a minute. That wasn't a play. That happened. Sort of like that. I was just telling a story.

ACTOR 4: Bingo, Kenneth. A story. That's all a play really is.

(Scene: Ancient Greece)

(Mysterious noise off-stage. The door opens and ACTOR 1 *stands in the doorway as the other actors go back to their benches.* ACTOR 1 *slowly walks in, leaving the door open.)*

*(*KENNETH *looks at the opened door and hesitates.)*

ACTOR 1: I hear it's your first play.

*(*KENNETH *nods, then looks back at the door.* ACTOR 1 *continues without even looking at* KENNETH.*)*

ACTOR 1: Go ahead. No one will stop you.

*(*KENNETH *moves to the door, but is stopped when* ACTOR 1 *begins to speak—to the audience at first.)*

ACTOR 1: The first time I was allowed to go the theater, I went with my father. He took his son.

KENNETH: *(Cheekily)* And when was that? Fifty years ago? *(He laughs at his joke and turns to go.)*

ACTOR 1: A little more. Say two thousand and four hundred years ago. Since you asked. In ancient Greece.

KENNETH: What? Two thousand...?

ACTOR 1: It was dark in my room when father came to wake me, and I was already awake. Waiting for him.

KENNETH: Wait a minute. Are you saying...?

ACTOR 1: *(Turns to* KENNETH*)* Yes.

KENNETH: You expect me to believe...?

ACTOR 1: Yes. *(He continues his story.)* I heard father's sandals slap against the stone. *(He makes the sound with his feet.)* A sound I remember as so comforting. *(He repeats the sound.)* The latch bolt turned. My father—who would soon fall ill, then die, though I

didn't know that then—my father stood, lantern in
hand, in my doorway, his long black shadow sweeping
back down the hall. Are you coming or going, Kenneth?
(*No response*) Suit yourself. (*Continues.*) Father and I set
off, and still it was night, through the fogged winter
streets of Athens, lanterns, blankets, packed lunch.
Father let me hold the tokens pressed with the shape of
rabbits which allowed us admission into the theater.

KENNETH: Why rabbits?

ACTOR 1: I don't know. It's just what I remember.
We weren't the first to arrive. Crowds gathered at the
entrance. Crows hopped near some rotting garbage.
In the black morning, other men's voices seemed utterly
mysterious, as if they came not out of faces, but from
inside bellies, hollowed, echoing. Others began to
move and we followed. (*Without looking at* KENNETH)
Would you shut the door, Kenneth. There's a draft.

(KENNETH *hesitates, looks at the door, then goes to it and
shuts it. As Actor 1 hears it shut, he continues his story.*)

ACTOR 1: We took places very near the stage and to the
left. The angle of the seat made you turn your whole
body to see the stage.

(ACTOR 1 *turns and sees* KENNETH *still standing there.*)

ACTOR 1: Sit down, Kenneth. Make yourself
comfortable.

(*He continues as* KENNETH *hesitates, then goes and sits on
the ground near* ACTOR 1 *and listens.*)

ACTOR 1: Father laid out the blanket as the marble was
cold and wet with dew. I stood and looked back—
across the whole theater. What with the darkness and
the hundreds of glowing lanterns, it seemed like a
universe, a night sky, another world.
The man next to me tried to take up half my place, and
he wasn't that fat, just one of those pushy people. I set

my elbow at an angle, waited, then as he slid even
closer, he ran into my pointed bone. He got the point,
so to speak.

(KENNETH *laughs*.)

ACTOR 1: I got some of my room back.
A flute noise turned my eyes to the stage. Then a
trumpet. And another—in the distance, approaching.
And then, most wondrously, the sun began to rise
above the stage, from behind a distant hill, and it was as
if life itself, day, had made its entrance upon the stage.
And so the play began.
It was a comedy. I'd been told this. And about the
masks the actors wore—dark for men, lighter for
women. Though they were larger, more angular,
stranger than I'd imagined.
Two men arrived on stage from a door in the back wall.
They spoke. My neighbour laughed. Why? I laughed
too. When father did.
From above—oh, I remember this—a bird flew down...

KENNETH: *(Interrupting)* A bird!?

ACTOR 1: A man dressed as a bird, then another and
another—their sound as they flew down from so high.
I could see string attached to their backs, but that didn't
matter. Strings attached to magical birds dressed in
colours brighter than any clothes I'd ever seen.
And all of a sudden, the whole sun was out, it was
full morning, and bugs, bees hummed, smelling the
lunches, the funny men speaking words that made our
whole world laugh! And one bird—he flew so close to
me—landed right in front of me. As he sang...

KENNETH: Sang?

ACTOR 1: —these birds sang—I could see the spittle out
of his mask, and on his legs, the hairs, and wiggling
lines of falling sweat. I watched everything!
When half way through the clouds opened—real

clouds—and it rained, a bird slipped on the stage and fell, father using the blanket protected me as if I were in a tent, watching out of the open flap—the stage and the play. There was thunder—no that was later—and it came not from the sky—it was sunny again—but from a large metal bowl—it was silver—full of rolling rocks and stones. But it was thunder! It was real! Even with the sun shining!

And when three gods appeared upon a chariot—not through a door but from a cloud—I thought I'd die. The chariot bounced along a string and arrived, and I watched. There were more trumpets. And laughter. And father let me lean against his side. And even though I understood nothing—I was seven years old!—I felt everything. (Beat) Since then I've learned when I watch a play to see the wires on the chariot. The wigs on the masks of the gods. I know how the writer wrote what he did. And why. And I laugh at all the jokes, with everyone else.

Sometimes now I wish I didn't. Sometimes I wish we just wouldn't talk about it. Some things, I think, are best not understood. But we have no choice—we grow up.

(ACTOR 1 goes to KENNETH.)

ACTOR 1: That's enough rest. We should get back to your journey, Kenneth.

KENNETH: My...journey? Where am I going?

ACTOR 1: Into the heart and soul of the play.

(Scene: Henry V)

(ACTOR 1 leads KENNETH out through the door, closing it shut behind him. Immediately, a loud noise.)

(KENNETH and ACTOR 1 return through the door as the other actors on the benches begin to create loud sounds of war, of bombs dropping, buildings being blown up, people screaming, air raid sirens blasting, planes overhead.)

(KENNETH *looks around, confused.*)

KENNETH: Is this the foyer?

ACTOR 1: (*Shouting over the noise of battle*) Kenneth, this is World War II and we're in London during the Blitz. Bombs are dropping. Your country is under attack!

(ACTOR 4 *stands on the bench.*)

ACTOR 1: You wander into a theater.

(ACTOR 5 *brings on a chair center stage.*)

ACTOR 1: And this is what you hear.

ACTOR 4: (*Henry V*)
Once more unto the breach, dear friends, once more
Or close the wall up with our English dead!

KENNETH: What's this?

ACTOR 1: (*Explaining to* KENNETH:) It's from a play by Shakespeare, called Henry V. In the play the King of England urges his soldiers to fight on.

ACTOR 4: (*Henry V*)
In peace there's nothing so becomes a man
As modest stillness and humility,
But when the blast of war blows in our ears,
Then imitate the action of the tiger:

ACTOR 1: Thousands of good British men, women and children have died in London alone. Buildings burn. Bombs explode. The Nazis continue their assault! Will Britain surrender?!

ACTOR 4: (*Henry V*)
Stiffen the sinews, summon up the blood,
Disguise fair nature with hard-favoured rage.
Then lend the eyes a terrible aspect:
Let it pry through the portage of the head
Like the brass cannon let the brow o'er whelm it—!

(Over the continuing noise of war, ACTOR 5 *hurries to* KENNETH, *miming holding out a microphone to interview him.)*

ACTOR 5: Kenneth, how did that make you feel? Such heroism! Such a speech, while your country is being attacked!?

KENNETH: Uh—good. *(Taken with the emotion)* I think, if I were feeling scared, it's the kind of thing I'd want to hear. To fight back. To not give in. *(Shouts.)* To win the war!!

(Silence)

ACTOR 1: Now, Kenneth, listen—It's nearly thirty years later. We are in the 1960s—and another war is going on—far away in Asia, in a place called Vietnam. *(Beat)* Millions of young people protest against this war, in marches across America and Britain and around the world. They march, singing,

(One ACTOR *begins to sing* We Shall Overcome. *Others join in after first line.)*

ACTOR 1: candles flickering, like waves of bright dots, breakers in an ocean of people. There are prayers for the war to end. And you, Kenneth, wander again into that same theater, and hear the same speech, spoken by the same actor in the same way.

(Singing turns to humming.)

ACTOR 4: *(Henry V)*
Once more unto the breach, dear friends, once more
Or close the wall up with our English dead!
In peace there's nothing so becomes a man
As modest stillness and humility...

ACTOR 1: In Vietnam armies have slaughtered women and children. On television you've seen whole villages massacred by soldiers. The killing has to stop!

ACTOR 4: *(Henry V)*
But when the blast of war blows in our ears,
Then imitate the action of the tiger;
Stiffen the sinews, summon up the blood,
Disguise fair nature with hard-favored rage.

(ACTOR 5 again hurries to KENNETH *with a microphone.)*

ACTOR 5: Kenneth, how did that make you feel? Such boasting from a general as armies slaughter women and children?!

KENNETH: *(Hesitates)* Uh—I didn't like it. I didn't like him. *(Points to Henry V.)* It sounded so—loud. So—thoughtless.

(Humming stops. ACTOR 4 *sits.)*

ACTOR 1: The same play, Kenneth, the same words spoken the same way—but they feel like totally different plays. One is heroic. Wonderful. One, just "loud". Why is that, Kenneth?

KENNETH: *(Confused, shaking his head)* I don't know.

ACTOR 5: Because of you, Kenneth. Because of what you bring to a play, to watching it. Because of who you are, because of what is happening in your world.

KENNETH: Because of me?

ACTOR 2: *(From bench)* Without you, Kenneth, there would be no play. Without your thoughts, without your experiences and your feelings.

KENNETH: Without me?

ACTOR 3: *(From bench)* You change it by who you are. You create it by watching, by being there.

KENNETH: Me?

ACTOR 1: Kenneth, the play—*is* you.

(Scene: Shakespeare's Day)

(KENNETH *is absorbed by this idea. He stands as he lets the idea sink in.* ACTOR 1 *returns to a bench as* ACTOR 5 *takes chair off and sits on it, upstage behind the door frame.*)

(KENNETH *looks around and realizes he is alone.*)

(*Beat*)

(*Behind him the door opens.* ACTOR 4 *and* ACTOR 2 *enter. They mime as if they were in an actors' dressing room [e.g. removing make-up], looking into an imaginary mirror off stage left.*)

(KENNETH, *still on the floor, watches as* ACTOR 4 *looks at himself in the imaginary mirror, then turns to go back out.*)

KENNETH: (*Stopping him*) I—uh liked that speech you made.

ACTOR 4: (*Offended*) I thought you found it—loud and...thoughtless.

KENNETH: Oh, you heard that.
I liked it the first—.

(*Door slams.* ACTOR 4 *is gone.*)

KENNETH: —time.

(ACTOR 2 *turns from the imaginary mirror towards the audience.*)

ACTOR 2: First play?

(KENNETH, *confused, looks behind himself—who is she talking to?*)

ACTOR 2: It's your first play, isn't it, Kenneth?

(*He hesitates, then nods.*)

ACTOR 2: Lucky you. (*Beat*) I remember the first time I went to see a play.

KENNETH: (*As a joke*) When was that? Twenty, thirty...?

ACTOR 2: Almost exactly...four hundred years ago.

KENNETH: Oh.

ACTOR 2: I was living with my Uncle and Aunt
near Moorgate. My parents were dead. I don't even
remember them. Uncle was a hired man at the theater.
Aunt, a cleaner there. I was no more than... five, when
they started taking—no, carrying me on my Aunt's
back—through the crowds across Blackfriars—the
beggars, the dirt and the noise—and to the theater.
We'd slip in a side door because we didn't have to pay.
Aunt grabbed a place in the pit where she thought
I could see best. Up close, so even if I got tired of
standing, I could always sit on her feet, look up and
see—something. Like the clouds floating above us.
Then the doors would open and in came the crowds
of audience—into the pit with us, kicking up dirt,
pushing. Aunt was good at pushing back. They were
all around us, in seats, under roofs, behind railings. Up
a level, then up a level again. Looking down upon us.
I remember the actors' clothes, the colors...brighter than
anything I'd ever seen before. Except perhaps at the
Fair near Moorfields.
The plays, I don't remember. I'm sure I couldn't
understand much. Aunt would ask if I could see.
Once an actor came right to the edge of the stage,
inches from my face, so that I could see the scratches
on his boots. When he spoke—and he did quite
loudly—I looked down, shyly away. He was too close.·
The sword fights were always my favorite.
Aunt let me eat an apple during the parts that were
very confusing and boring.
Uncle would have to sit above the actors, with the
other musicians. He played a drum. I couldn't see him—
only the bottom of the drum.
Sometimes it rained and we pushed toward the sides to
get a little under the roofs. Sometimes it was sunny and
hot. One very hot day, Aunt rubbed my legs with a cool
damp cloth as I watched. I can still feel that.

It was after one of these visits—and Uncle has told
me many, many times, he never tires of telling the
story—that the most extraordinary event happened.
The play, which play I don't know, had been over
maybe an hour or so. I'd fallen asleep—on Aunt's coat
while she cleaned. And then I awoke... I awoke and
before me—the audience, of course, had all gone—
on the stage was now set a table, a few chairs, and,
as it was now later in the afternoon, a few candles had
been lit and burned and glowed.
The actors, no longer in their bright clothes, sat or stood
or talked, when in walked—Uncle swears I was there—
in walked Mr Shakespeare, the writer of plays. I don't
remember what he looked like. Uncle never said.
But he had papers in his hands, which he then began
to hand out—copies, Uncle said, of a play.
Mr Shakespeare spoke: "Since the Admiral's Men"—
another group of actors—"Since the Admiral's Men
have made such a success with their *Robin Hood* play—"
Actors shook their heads, grumbled. Some had seen it
and didn't like it. "I thought," he continued, "I would
write one myself, set in a forest."
And the four or five copies of the play were spread out
along the table and the actors stood, grouped
themselves around each copy—to share. The candle
light hitting the white papers—making them appear
to glow.
And so—according to Uncle—I sat, aged five, and
listened—the only person in the whole pit—as these
actors read—for the first time ever—for the first time to
Mr Shakespeare's ears, believed Uncle—this play about
love, and a girl dressed as a boy, that I have since seen
countless times, and even acted in twice, called *As You
Like It*.
Actors read, there was some laughter. Uncle said he
laughed himself from the musicians' balcony where he
was polishing instruments. Clouds passed above. It got

dark. Then it was night. And I was there in that dark building witnessing these men—of course, then they were men, no women—the youngest man played the girl called Rosalind—watching them read and discover and explore—what no one had ever read or discovered or explored before.
Uncle swears, I was there.

(Scene: Pretend)

(Beat. Three knocks at the door as ACTOR 2 *sits on a bench to one side.)*

(Door opens to a strange noise. ACTOR 5 *comes on and pretends to clean up the dressing room; she "sweeps".)*

ACTOR 5: *(As a caretaker)* Could you move please.

*(*KENNETH *picks up one foot, then the other as* ACTOR 5 *goes on "sweeping".* ACTOR 5 *"sweeps"* KENNETH *around the stage.)*

KENNETH: *(To* ACTOR 5:*)* Did you know that a play's a story? *(Then proudly)* And a play is—me? I'll bet you didn't.

ACTOR 5: Is that it? Is that all a play is?

KENNETH: Why? Is there more? Is there? What else is a play?

ACTOR 5: *(Pointing to "nothing")* Is that crisp packet yours? Pick it up.

KENNETH: *(Looking, confused)* What—?

ACTOR 5: Kenneth, it's not polite to drop litter.

KENNETH: But I don't see...

ACTOR 5: Kenneth—

KENNETH: *(Hesitates, then, suddenly getting it, picks up the imaginary crisp packet)* Pretend! Pretend! A play is also pretend. I knew that!

ACTOR 5: When people say a play has a certain style, what they're saying is, it has a certain way to pretend.

(Hands KENNETH *the "broom".* KENNETH *takes it and turns it into something else [e.g. a pool cue])*

ACTOR 5: Of course there are different ways to pretend.

KENNETH: Oh.

*(*STAGE MANAGER *bursts through the door, shouting:)*

STAGE MANAGER: Everyone on stage for three different ways to pretend!

(Scene: Playground)

*(*ACTORS *stand immediately;* ACTOR 4, *with a whistle round his neck, "hands out" imaginary scripts.* KENNETH *hands "broom" to audience member.)*

ACTOR 4: Who needs a script? Take a script. *(Et cetera)*

(The others speak at the same time as they take the scripts: "I need one", "me too", "oh this is the boring bit", "I don't think so" et cetera.)

ACTOR 4: *(Has taken a "script" and "reads" to* KENNETH:) It's a bright sunny day. *(Stops.)* Or would you rather read the stage directions?

*(*KENNETH *hesitates, looks at the "script", then:)*

KENNETH: Uh—no. You read them.

ACTOR 4: *("Reading")* Not a cloud in the sky. We're in a school playground. Lunchtime.

(Terrific noise from the ACTORS *who suddenly become kids at play. The noise is cut dead as* ACTOR 4 *blows his whistle. Kids freeze.)*

ACTOR 4: *(To* KENNETH*)* It's the day of the big match between England and Brazil. *(Or other appropriate names)*

(The ACTORS *start shouting to each other.)*

ACTORS: *(Choosing their favorite players)* "I'll be Gazza", "I'll be Seaman". "I wanna be Seaman. " "I'll be Shearer" *(Et cetera).*

(Another whistle blast cuts the noise dead. Kids freeze again.)

ACTOR 4: These kids know the names of all the players, their positions, the statistics, everything. The players—well, they're heroes. And out here—England always wins.

KENNETH: What part do I play?

(ACTOR pretends to throw a ball up in the air. All look up.)

ACTOR 4: You? You're Brazil!

(ACTOR 4 kicks an imaginary ball high in the air. The imaginary ball falls. The ACTORS and KENNETH begin an imaginary game of football in the playground. KENNETH "fouls" ACTOR 5 and brings her down.)

(Another whistle blast. The ACTORS go into slow motion, very exaggerated, imitating football players reacting to a foul in the penalty box as ACTOR 5 gives a running commentary on her own actions.)

ACTOR 5: Oh no, my God, Gascoigne *(Or appropriate name.)* has been brought down in the penalty box. He looks to be in terrible pain. Blood's pouring down his leg. They're calling for a stretcher. No. Wait. He's standing up. He's on his feet. He's limping, but he looks O K to play. He's going to carry on. Gascoigne is going to take the penalty himself!

(The ACTORS make throbbing sounds as ACTOR 4 places the ball on the penalty spot.)

(KENNETH stands in goal in front of the audience. ACTOR 5 takes the penalty in slow motion and scores. The others, still in slow motion, cheer, jump et cetera on ACTOR 5. Silent roar while ACTOR 4 blows the whistle.)

ACTOR 4: Everyone pretends together, Kenneth.
We share a pretend story, a pretend world. Everyone—
our characters—are all larger than life, all heroes,
gods even. This is the sort of pretend you can find
in an ancient Greek play, Kenneth.

KENNETH: A Greek play...

ACTOR 4: When the ancient Greeks went to the theater,
they went to share a story, to pretend together.

(Scene: Kenneth's Home)

(The STAGE MANAGER *makes a loud sound.* KENNETH
*turns and looks out into the auditorium as the other actors
carry a bench on and sit like a family portrait.)*

*(*KENNETH *turns back as he asks:)*

KENNETH: Where are we now?   ·

ACTOR 4: Don't you recognize it?

*(*KENNETH *looks at the family portrait. Shakes his head)*

ACTOR 4: We're at your house, Kenneth. There's your
sister's boyfriend, George.

(Points to ACTOR 2 *who imitates George and waves at*
KENNETH*)*

ACTOR 4: You remember him. There's your sister Ruth.

(Points to ACTOR 1 *who imitates Ruth.)*

ACTOR 4: Your little sister Pat.

(Points to ACTOR 5 *who imitates Pat.)*

ACTOR 5: *(As Pat)* Will you stop chewing gum in my
ear, Kenneth.

KENNETH: Kenneth?

ACTOR 4: And that's you.

*(*ACTOR 3 *pretends to take out a can and opens it as*
KENNETH *did at the start of the play.)*

KENNETH: Yep. That's me all right.

ACTOR 2: *(As George)* I thought there was going to be something to eat....

ACTOR 1: *(As Ruth)* Do you like my hair like this?

ACTOR 2: *(As George)* Where's the food?

ACTOR 1: *(As Ruth)* I used to wear it long.

ACTOR 3: *(As* KENNETH*)* Where am I supposed to sit? Move over.

ACTOR 1: *(As Ruth, to Actor 3)* Will you stop pushing?

ACTOR 3: *(As* KENNETH*)* What's the time?

ACTOR 5: *(As Pat)* Can I put nail polish on too?

ACTOR 1: *(As Ruth, turning to George showing her fingernails)* What color do you like? Black or purple?

(George belches/scratches backside.)

ACTOR 4: It's later the same day. And the England-Brazil match has already begun. I'm your T V.

*(*ACTOR 4 *becomes the T V.)*

KENNETH: And me? Who am I? *(He asks* ACTOR 4 *and stands in the way of the T V.)*

ALL: Get out of the way

ACTOR 5: Who do you want to be?

*(*KENNETH *thinks for a second, then has a fantastic idea.)*

KENNETH: My mother.

ACTOR 5: Then that's who you are.

KENNETH: Yes!

*(*ACTOR 4 *begins a commentary, low.* KENNETH, *getting into his new role, interrupts.)*

KENNETH: *(As a force of nature, patrolling the stage)* Get those feet off my sofa! What are we, animals? Is this a zoo? Tell me, is my home now a zoo? Because that's how it looks to me. Pick up those crumbs. What, we don't eat with plates anymore? Someone throw away all the plates? Or are they still piled three feet high in the sink waiting for one of you kids to get the hint and wash them up? I can't do everything. I try. Lord knows, I try. I'd do anything for you children. *(Suddenly to George)* Get your hands off her. I slave for you. I cook. Look at these hands! And what do I ask in return?! I know what would really make my day—a nice cuppa tea.

*(*KENNETH *goes out the door—to the kitchen. The kids change their behavior momentarily until "Mum" returns.)*

ACTOR 4: *(As T V, under* KENNETH, *uninterrupted)* What a good game the England captain is having. Inspirational. Adams pushes the ball out to Ince, who slips the ball to Gascoigne.

*(*KENNETH *returns with a "cup" of tea; He/she leans against the door frame and mumbles, pretending to drink the imaginary tea.)*

KENNETH: Football, football, football. Don't you ever get tired of watching football?

ACTOR 4: This looks promising for England. Can they pull something out of the hat at the last moment?

*(*KENNETH *makes a big gesture of looking at his/her watch.)*

KENNETH: Isn't it about time for Coronation Street? *(Or appropriate name. He goes to T V.)*

ACTOR 4: Gazza dummies, switches play to the right. He's found McManaman—.

KENNETH: Will you look at that dust.

(KENNETH *dusts the screen, others move heads to try and see.*)

ACTOR 4: *(Continuing)* He's going down the line.
He's passed his man. MacManaman gets his cross in.

(Excitement grows amongst those watching.)

KENNETH: Are we on the right side?

ACTOR 4: The ball goes high, and—the goalie's missed
it, but the cross is too high for Shearer too. *(Groans)*
It looks like we're headed for the dreaded—

(KENNETH *[As Mum] changes the T V channel. Panic
among the kids.* KENNETH *[As Mum] changes the channel
back.*)

ACTOR 4: —penalty shoot out.

KENNETH: Oh, were you watching something?
Oh sorry. Pardon me...wouldn't want you to miss
a single fun-filled second.

(Groans and nail biting from the kids.)

ACTOR 5: *(No longer Pat)* Watching a football match is
just another kind of pretend, Kenneth.

KENNETH: You talking to me? *(He looks at the T V and
slowly starts to get interested in it.)*

(The ACTORS *begin a series of shouts of "yes" as indicated.)*

*(Each shout accompanies a successful England penalty.
The shouts start low and build to a climax.)*

ACTOR 5: *(Next to* KENNETH*)* As we watch we pretend
that the match is all that matters in the world.

ACTORS: Yes!

ACTOR 5: We block out everything else. We lose
ourselves in the drama.

(KENNETH *[As Mum] has lost himself in the drama.*)

KENNETH: What, dear? I wasn't listening.

KENNETH & ACTORS: Yes!

ACTOR 2: *(Not as George)* A Shakespeare play pretends like this. What is going to happen next? Who's going to win? Who's going to die?

KENNETH & ACTORS: Yes!!

ACTOR 3: A Greek audience knew the stories before they came to see a play.

ACTORS: Yes!

ACTOR 5: The audience for Shakespeare came to be surprised. They came to be excited. They came expecting to lose themselves in the play.

KENNETH & ACTORS: Yes—ssssss.

ACTOR 5: *(Over this)* To express themselves, to express emotions that we don't often get the chance to express in our everyday lives.

(The final "Yes" turns to despair, groans, and the kids slump as the penalty is missed.)

ACTOR 2: *(As George,stunned)* We lost.

(KENNETH [As Mum] has covered her face. She can't look.)

ACTOR 5: This is another kind of pretend.

(Scene: After the Match)

(ACTOR 4 blows his whistle wearily and with sadness. The kids all suddenly lie around complaining, slumped over one another.)

ACTOR 1: *(As Ruth)* I'm tired.

ACTOR 2: *(As George)* I'm hungry.

ACTOR 5: *(As Pat)* I'm bored.

ACTOR 3: *(As KENNETH)* Will you stop lying on me?

ACTOR 5: *(As Pat)* Where am I supposed to put my foot?

KENNETH: Where are we now—the England changing room?

ACTOR 4: No, we're still in your house. The match is over. Everyone's tired. Grumpy.

ACTOR 3: *(As KENNETH)* Get off!

ACTOR 4: Hungry.

ACTOR 2: *(As George)* Can we order pizza?

ACTOR 4: Whingeing.

ACTOR 1: *(As Ruth)* Will you stop making that sound with your mouth?

ACTOR 4: But do they admit it?

KENNETH: *(As Mum)* You should be off to bed.

ALL: *(Variously)* We're not tired. We're fine. What's on T V?

ACTOR 1: *(As Ruth)* Let's all do our homework!

ACTOR 4: They *are* tired, aren't they?

(KENNETH [As Mum] nods, looking at them.)

ACTOR 4: But they're pretending that they're not. They feel one thing, but say another.

KENNETH: *(As Mum:)* You mean lie? I'll wash their mouths out with—.

ACTOR 5: *(As Pat)* No, not lie. Pretend.

(The kids turn to Mum and explain.)

ACTOR 2: *(As George)* It's what we do everyday. What we do at school.

KENNETH: *(As Mum)* You do, do you?

ACTOR 2: *(As George)* What our parents do at work.

ACTOR 1: *(As Ruth)* We do it at home. At dinner with you and Dad.

KENNETH: *(As Mum)* If I catch you doing it again—!

ACTOR 3: *(As KENNETH)* It's what I do with my sisters upstairs in our rooms.

(Turns to Ruth, who is being held by George)

ACTOR 3: *(As KENNETH)* I hate you, I hope you die! *(Turns back and explains.)* She won't turn her music down!

ACTOR 5: *(As Pat)* We say things which we don't really feel. You do it too, Mum.

KENNETH: *(Incredulous)* Are you saying I lie???

ACTOR 1: *(As Ruth)* I think George is really wonderful, don't you mum?

("She" is holding George [ACTOR 2]. "He" smiles at Mum and belches.)

KENNETH: Yes, dear. Lovely.

ACTOR 5: *(Repeating)* You see, Mum. We all say things we don't feel.

ACTOR 3: *(As KENNETH)* And this is the kind of pretend, Mum, you can find in a Chekhov play.

(All turn in amazement and stare at ACTOR 3.)

ACTORS: A what?

KENNETH: *(As Mum)* A—"Chekhov" *(Having trouble with the name.)* play??

ACTOR 3: In a Chekhov play there are no heroes. People are—well, like us. A little confused, a little lost. Like our family.

KENNETH: *(As Mum)* There's nothing wrong with our—. *(And suddenly turns on "Kenneth".)* And you, young man, mister smarty pants, how come you know so much about a-, a-, any play?

(She laughs. The rest of the family laughs too.)

ACTOR 3: *(As* KENNETH*)* I've been trying to tell you all day, Mum, I went to see this play. I had to—go to the toilet—I went through the wrong door—.

KENNETH: *(As Mum, yawning)* Kenneth, that's nice dear. Tell me another time. Will you look at this mess. There are crumbs everywhere. What am I raising, animals?

ACTOR 3: *(As* KENNETH, *hurt)* Mum? Don't you want to hear what happened to me?

KENNETH: *(As Mum, looking around)* Who's going to clean this mess up? *(To "Kenneth")* Kenneth, not now. Later. I'll do the hoovering.

ACTOR 3: *(As* KENNETH*)* Mum?!!!

(She looks at him, then goes back to giving orders.)

KENNETH: *(As Mum)* Ruth, you take the dog out. George, pick up the glasses and plates. Pat, start the washing up in the kitchen.

*(*ACTOR 3, *who is still pretending to be* KENNETH, *storms out, angry, slamming the door behind him/her. The other* ACTORS *exit without going through the door.)*

KENNETH: *(As Mum)* And Kenneth—where's Kenneth? Where'd that boy go now? He's never around when I need him. Kenneth?!!! *(Shouting)* Kenneth?!!!

(Scene: Moscow)

("She" goes to the door, looks out, then goes out, still calling "Kenneth". The door closes, immediately opens, and KENNETH, *now back as* KENNETH, *angry and hurt, hurries into his room.)*

(From behind the door, ACTOR 1 *imitates* KENNETH/Mum's *shouting and picks up where* KENNETH *as Mum had left off.)*

ACTOR 1 *(As Mum, from behind the door)* Kenneth! Kenneth, don't you run away from me!

KENNETH: What a pair of lungs she's got.

ACTOR 1: Do you want your pocket money or not?!!

KENNETH:*(To us)* Why are parents like that? They're like a—*(He thinks.)*—a splinter. They get under your skin. At first it just hurts a little, then it starts to get red, swells up, turns mushy and white and then green.

ACTOR 1: Kenneth!

KENNETH: *(Turns and shouts back)* I hate you! I hope you die?!!

(ACTOR 1, as Mum, bursts open the door and shouts at KENNETH *in his room.)*

ACTOR 1: I heard that! Don't you dare talk to me like that!!

*(*KENNETH *runs to the door and slams it shut in Mum's face.* ACTOR 1 *bangs on the door.)*

ACTOR 1: Unlock this door immediately, Kenneth! Just you wait until your father gets home. He'll have plenty to say to you about this. You're in big trouble, my boy!

*(*KENNETH *has cowered with his hands over his ears as his Mum is pounding and shouting. Then he realizes:)*

KENNETH: It's only a play. *(To us)* It's only a play! It's only... *(Goes to door and opens it. Mum has gone.)* ...a play. Phew. I thought I was in real trouble there.

*(*ACTOR 3 *carries on a bench.)*

KENNETH: Excuse me. But this is my room. You can't just walk in here...

ACTOR 3: Your room, Kenneth? This isn't your room. This is a theater.

(ACTORS 2, 4 *and* 5, *now as older teenagers, enter through the door and sit on the bench, looking straight out front. They leave a place in the middle for* KENNETH.)

ACTOR 2: *(Rubbing her arms)* Moscow's so cold in the winter.

KENNETH: Moscow? Russia?

ACTOR 2: Where did you think you were?

(Others laugh.)

ACTOR 4: *(To* KENNETH*)* But the theaters...feel...they keep them so warm. So one minute you're outside and it's cold. Then the next you're inside and you're hot. It's like they want you to fall asleep.

KENNETH: *(Confused)* This is Moscow?

ACTOR 5: Why? Is there somewhere else you'd rather be?

(Door opens and ACTOR 1 *stands there as Mum.)*

ACTOR 1: And you, young man, can stay in your room until you apologise. *(Slams door shut.)*

KENNETH: *(To* ACTOR 5*)* No. Moscow's fine.

*(*KENNETH *joins the others on the bench, taking his place as if in a row of seats in a theater.)*

ACTOR 3: I always fall asleep in the theater. *(Yawns)* Shakespeare plays are the worst.

(Everyone agrees except KENNETH.*)*

ACTOR 3: I'm out in seconds with them. And then they go on and on and on ...

KENNETH: Well, no. Shake...

ACTOR 3: *(Ignoring his interruption)* Why bother?

ACTOR 5: She's right. Why live in the past?

ACTOR 2:What is so fascinating about sitting in the dreary dark, watching a bunch of people dressed up in funny old-fashioned costumes—and the colors are so ugly—speaking nonsense. Who cares? None of it has anything to do with my life.

ACTOR 4: The world outside those theater doors is a lot more interesting—a lot more exciting and real. Things happen out there.

ACTOR 2: Ask any of us. Listen to us talking over coffee. We're twice as articulate as Shakespeare.

ACTOR 4: That's right.

ACTOR 3: Tell him.

ACTOR 5: It's true!

ACTOR 2: About what matters.

ACTOR 1: You just wait till your father gets home!

ACTOR 4: And when you go to see a play...

ACTOR 5: (Laughs) Dragged!

ACTOR 4: ...and there's someone our age in it. You have to wonder, has the writer ever even met a young person? They don't know what they're talking about.

ACTOR 2: They don't know me.

ACTOR 3: My mother took me to one play.

KENNETH: Your mother? When was this?

ACTOR 3: About...a hundred years ago.

KENNETH: Oh.

ACTOR 3: (Describing the play as if they are all watching it) In the beginning of the play, Constantine, a young man—like us—

ACTOR 5: I've seen this too. He's our age.

ACTOR 3: And he's trying to put on a play—one he's written. It's new, he says, and not old fashioned. Even I knew it wasn't very good. *(Others agree.)* But he was really young and he was trying to do something different. Then his mother makes fun of it.

ACTOR 2: Of him really.

ACTOR 3: She knows better.

ACTOR 5: She's an actress herself, his mother. She just laughs at him.

ACTOR 3: My mother had to sh-sh me—I suppose I'd started to say things out loud. I didn't hear myself. But it really did bother me. This young guy, her son, was only trying to so something for now. He was tired of everyone sticking their heads into the sand. But they just laughed, those old people. Old like my mother.

ACTOR 2: Everything he did, his mother had to pick apart.

(KENNETH *looks back toward the door and his Mum.*)

ACTOR 3: But I saw through her and all those tired old people, I saw how scared they really were of anything different. For them it was their way or nothing! Why don't they just die!!

ACTOR 1: *(As Mum, through door)* I heard that, Kenneth.

KENNETH: But I didn't say.... *(To others)* I didn't really mean....

ACTOR 5: And Nina, what they did to that poor young girl!

ACTOR 3: At the interval I didn't want to leave my seat, I was so angry. I didn't want it to stop. I wanted—I just felt that one of us—one of the young ones—was finally going to stand up to those old people and I was waiting to see that. *(Beat)* Mother brought me a small cake

during the interval. I didn't eat. I didn't want anything
from her. *(She is unable to go on.)*

ACTOR 5: *(To* KENNETH*)* The play was called *The Seagull.*

ACTOR 2: By the Russian playwright, Anton Chekhov.

ACTOR 5: The curtain at the theater had a design of a
seagull. Did anyone else notice that?

ACTOR 3: The lights went down again—they turned
down the gas in the lights along the wall—some
women. And...the young people didn't stand up for
themselves at all! I bit my lip. I started to hear things
I hear every day of my life, and I can't take them any
more!

ACTOR 1: *(As Mum)* Kenneth, I can hear your father
now.   -

ACTOR 3: Why do they think that young people can be
treated like that? Stop it!! Look out at the world—don't
you see that it's all changing?! You're killing your son,
lady!!

*(*ACTOR 4 *stands, goes behind* ACTOR 3 *and rubs her
shoulders as she talks.)*

ACTOR 5: And that man—the older writer—what a
sleaze. What he did to poor Nina. Made her fall in love
with him. He just played with her feelings. I know older
men like that.

ACTOR 4: Why do we take it?

ACTOR 3: Then at the end, the young
man—Constantine—
he leaves the room and goes into a room we can't
see—just through a door—you can see some of the
room when the door is opened, but he closes the door,
and then I hear a gun shot.

(All react as if to hearing the shot.)

ACTOR 3: No, it can't be! No! *(She covers her head.)*

ACTOR 2: *(To* KENNETH*)* The doctor goes into the other room and comes back and whispers to the old writer: the young man's shot himself. He's dead. Don't tell his mother.

ACTOR 3: *(Nearly in tears)* He's dead. And no one is crying! Not these old people. They don't care! They don't! Not about me!!!

ACTOR 4: *(To* KENNETH*)* But it was only a play. *(She wipes her eyes. Beat)* And as she said—she doesn't like plays. *(To* KENNETH*)* Do you, Kenneth?

(Three loud knocks on the door.)

ACTOR 2: That's for you, Kenneth.

*(*KENNETH *hesitates, then gets up and looks at the door. Three more knocks)*

ACTOR 2: Answer it, Kenneth. It's your room.

(He opens the door to reveal the STAGE MANAGER.*)*

STAGE MANAGER: Actors on stage, please. We're starting the play again. Everyone on stage.

(Scene: Epilogue)

(The ACTORS *immediately drop out of character and become actors, taking the bench off and picking up instruments et cetera, ready to exit through the door in order to start the play again. They ignore* KENNETH.*)*

ACTOR 4: I guess they found that boy. The one who got lost in the play.

ACTOR 5: They either found him or maybe they just made him part of the play.

ACTOR 2: Can they do that?

ACTOR 5: That's what happened to *(Name of* ACTOR 3*)*

ACTOR 3: Got lost and never left.

KENNETH: *(To* ACTOR 1*)* Got lost in the play forever???

ACTOR 4: He was a nice boy, did you talk to him?

ACTOR 2: I told him about the first time I went to see a play.

ACTOR 5: Nice kid.

ACTOR 2: I loved the story about his sister.

(They are all out of the door, except ACTOR 1, *who is standing in the doorway, about to follow the others through the door.)*

ACTOR 1: Are you coming, Kenneth?

*(*KENNETH *hesitates)*

KENNETH: What play are you...?

ACTOR 1: It's called *Kenneth's First Play.* Maybe you know it?

KENNETH: Is it a...Greek play? Or is it a Shakespeare play?

ACTOR 1: What are you talking about?

KENNETH: I know...it's a Chekhov play.

ACTOR 1: No, Kenneth. It's a new play. Written for today. About you.

KENNETH: Oh.

ACTOR 1: So...are you coming?

*(*KENNETH *hesitates.)*

ACTOR 1: You don't have to, you know. If you don't want to be in the play anymore...

KENNETH: But it's my story.

ACTOR 1: Kenneth, you don't have to be in the play for it still to be about you. So if you wish to go...(*Gestures toward the audience.*)

KENNETH: How do I get out there? I've been trying....

ACTOR 1: It's the easiest thing in the world. Look— (*He gestures.*) —there's no wall. No barrier. They're people. We're people. We're all in the same room.

KENNETH: You mean at any time I could have—?

ACTOR 1: Yes, of course. Is that your seat?

(KENNETH *nods and slowly goes to take his seat.*)

ACTOR 1: Are those crisps all over the floor? (*In the voice of Mum*) Kenneth? Crisps in a theater? (*He walks off the stage and takes a crisp—smells it*) Salt and vinegar. My favorite. (*To a person in the audience.*) Nice shirt.

(*He talks to the audience as the* ACTORS *begin the play again, leaving a gap in the middle for* ACTOR 1 *to join them when they have lined up. They do not hum a Greek chant this time.*)

(*He turns around and joins all the other* ACTORS *who line up as at the start of the play.*)

ACTOR 1: The play, historically, began...

KENNETH: (*Interrupting*) two thousand years ago!

ACTOR 1: (*Smiling*) ...with the ancient Greeks.

(ACTOR 4 *turns and makes his loud noise.*)

ACTOR 2: The play, many people believe, only came into its own four hundred years ago with the genius of....

KENNETH: (*Interrupting again*) William Shakespeare!

(ACTOR 5 *turns and makes her sound, as:*)

ACTOR 3: The play—as we know it today—it can be argued—derives from the Russian playwright...

KENNETH: Anton Chekhov!

ACTOR 3: ...who lived a mere one hundred years ago.

ACTOR 1: And this, our play...

KENNETH: My play!

ACTOR 3: Kenneth's First Play...

ACTOR 1: Began, today, here, with all of you.

END OF PLAY

COMMENTARY AND NOTES

Ways of Using the Play

KENNETH'S FIRST PLAY was launched by a
professional theater company but we always intended
it to be of use beyond the profession.

The aesthetic choices that lie behind the play are
deliberate rather than the result of economic problems,
although we were asked by a few audience members
why we could not afford to stage the play more
lavishly. The play lasts approximately 45 minutes.
There are no costumes and both the set—a door, two
benches and two chairs—and the props—a packet of
crisps, a can of drink, some musical instruments, and
a whistle—are minimal; it is the imaginations of the
performers and the audience that come together to
create the ever-changing reality on stage. Paradoxically,
the more "real" the actors could be as they played the
various characters allocated to them, even when quite
exaggerated, the more effective each moment and the
whole play became.

We always envisaged KENNETH'S FIRST PLAY as
being part of a larger exploration that involved an
illustrated book on the history of plays, a video, and a
C D-ROM as well as further short plays or musicals to
complement our first effort. It is possible, therefore, to
dismantle KENNETH'S FIRST PLAY and, depending
on age and intention, to use sections of it without
having to perform the whole thing.

To facilitate this, the text of the play has been divided

into sections, which, for ease of reference, have been
given appropriate names: Induction, In the Play, *Romeo
and Juliet*, Ancient Greece, *Henry V*, Shakespeare's Day,
Pretend, Playground, Kenneth's Home, After the
Match, Moscow, Epilogue.

The play and/or its constituent scenes can be used as
a teaching and learning resource most obviously in the
study of English or Drama, but there is cross-curricular
potential as well.

The Ancient Greece section or the Shakespeare's Day
section, could, for instance, be explored in a variety of
ways—as examples of storytelling or as introductions
to the drama of those two periods; in other subject
areas, particularly the Humanities, as a stimulation/
complementary activity to creating related artefacts
(e.g. a Greek mask), as source material for exploration
of the customs and habits of the two societies or as an
aid to understanding the role of empathy. The scene in
Kenneth's Home could be used in Personal and Social
Education as well as in English and Drama as the basis
for improvisation and role playing, with pupils/
students developing or changing the situation
themselves. The pupils/students could also write/
create their own scenarios/plays out of this or other
scenes.

There are many other possibilities for KENNETH'S
FIRST PLAY to fit into a lesson plan or Scheme of
Work, some of which are listed below.

The play is not age specific and neither are the roles
of the actors in it. Kenneth is a youthful, innocent and
enquiring spirit; Actor 1 turns out to be 2400 years old,
Actor 2 around 400 years old and Actor 3 about 100
years old, yet they also play children in a school
playground, Kenneth's sisters and his sister's
boyfriend, and much more besides.

There are six actors, three male, three female. There is
a dramatic and/or historical logic to the gender choices

behind the writing of the parts, yet it is possible to change the genders of the other actors if required, particularly if only one or two sections of the play are being used. It is possible to make the central role female (e.g. KATIE'S FIRST PLAY), with only a few changes to the text and without altogether losing the idea of role play and gender swapping. (We have listed our suggested changes in Appendix 1.).

Similarly, the sounds required by the text can be made by any suitable instruments or improvised objects, and other changes can be made as necessary (e.g. in the Playground/Home scenes, the home team —or even the sport—can be altered). Even vocabulary can be adjusted to take account of different linguistic usage. (North American variations are listed in Appendix 2.)

Issues/Themes

The main question asked in KENNETH'S FIRST PLAY is, "what is a play?". Kenneth learns that, as with so much in life, there is no simple answer. He discovers that a play is several things:

a play is a story
a play is himself, i.e. the audience, and
a play is pretend.

But he also discovers that there are different ways of telling a story in play form, different audiences and theatrical experiences, and different ways to pretend, different styles of playwriting.

He finds out that plays were written more than two thousand years ago and that plays and play-going have changed with the times. They are different in each of the three periods he visits —ancient Greece, Elizabethan England, Chekhov's Moscow—as well as today, in the present. His own experience of play-going and of a contemporary play—his own story told in play form—makes the historical story of plays an open-ended one; after all, every play, whether by Chekhov, Shakespeare or Sophocles, was a new play once, and, for someone seeing a play for the first time, even if it is hundreds of years old, it still is a new play.

Kenneth's journey through the play offers him an understanding of the complexity of how we communicate, interpret and make meanings. A moment in *Romeo and Juliet* catches his sister's attention because it relates directly to her own experience of meeting her boyfriend in the auditorium. Kenneth understands *Henry V* in different ways depending on the context in which he is seeing it; brave and heroic at a time of resistance to fascism; loud and empty at a time of imperial slaughter. Playing his mum, he is confronted with the difference between lying and pretence; we don't always mean what we say or say what we mean, a situation that develops in the Moscow scene.

This shows that meanings are not only made literally; it introduces the notion of sub-text in drama, and, with other episodes, shows that meanings can be made through images too. Furthermore, various sections show that meanings come not just through words but through other "languages" that are at work in a play, such as sound, gesture, movement. How these languages are all mixed together and understood in the crucible of the audiences' imaginations is what makes each visit to the theater unique.

Actor 1, however, offers a reflection on our attempts to analyse all these elements of the drama, which is not a plea for obfuscation but a yearning for a fuller, deeper sense of consciousness. "Some things, I think, are best not understood," he says, having found his enjoyment of theater somewhat blunted by his knowledge of its rules and practices. "But we have no choice—we grow up." And that is what Kenneth begins to do during the course of the play.

The text plays with theatricality, changing style and tone as quickly as it changes location. Kenneth is mysteriously propelled through a door and immediately enters a new world. The door is the entrance to and opening up of new adventure for Kenneth but it can also be a closing down of an escape route, for instance, in the second scene where he feels trapped as if in prison. Knocking on the door can herald a new beginning or frighten him (as, for example, an expression of parental wrath and portent of punishment to come).

The "fourth wall" convention is challenged directly at the very start and end of the play as Kenneth comes out from and then returns to the audience. These moments form part of the play's vigorous investigation of pretence—the pretence of character, time and setting, of illusion and reality, and, most importantly, of style and form—that is sustained throughout, as Kenneth and the other actors change period, location, gender, role, and age. This strand of the play provides not only an insight into how plays work but also into the difference between live drama in theater and the drama most people see, which is shown on television, video or film. .

For those who have training as actor-teachers or theater-in-education skills, the play can be adapted in a number of ways to that experience. The play already contains elements of different teaching modes (e.g. instruction, enquiry, empathy, drama) and it can be explored further in any, or combinations, of them. Kenneth and the other actors can be put in the "hot seat" to discover motive and characterisation. Moments in the play (e.g. in the Playground or in Kenneth's Home) can become physically as well as imaginatively "inter-active" and taken in participatory directions.

Kenneth could be taken on new adventures in which the outcomes are decided by the pupils/students.

Topics for class/Homework

(in discussion and/or written form):

What is a play?

Why do we tell stories about ourselves in play form?

What is the difference between time in a play and time in everyday life?

How is a play in the theater different from a story told on television, video or film?

What can be learned from a man playing a woman and vice versa in a play?

How can the same actor be different ages, gender and characters in the same play?

Act out a moment from a Shakespeare play you are studying:
  a) like the *Romeo and Juliet* scene, improvising/revising the situation of Ruth and George so that what they *see* on stage in some way reflects what is happening to them (and adding in others if desired);
  b) like the *Henry V* scene, improvising/revising the situation of Actor 1 and Kenneth (and adding in others in desired) so that what Kenneth "sees" on stage in some way reflects what is happening in society either now and/or at some other time.

How does what is happening in society affect what is happening on stage?

Talk/write about your first visit to a theater.

Find out about drama in non-English speaking cultures; in what ways are they the same, and in what ways different, from English-speaking drama.

What was it like to go to the theater in a) ancient
Greece, b) Shakespeare's time, c) Chekhov's time,
d) now?

Compare and contrast the different types of storytelling
in play form of the ancient Greeks (hero-based), the
Elizabethan/Jacobean period (centred on a new rising
class) and modern times (centred on "ordinary" people).

Look at different ways in which plays pretend and at
how "pretend" in a play works (e.g. the pretence of
character, time and location; illusion and reality; what
we mean by style and form.)

In the theatrical experience, what is the importance of
language; what is the importance of sub-text; what is
the nature and contribution of performance?

Curriculum Opportunities

Here are some examples of how KENNETH'S FIRST
PLAY could be used as a resource in a lesson plan or
Scheme of Work. (The U S equivalents are approximate.)

Ages 7-11 (Key Stage 2; Elementary School)

Activity: An introduction to storytelling in drama and to
what a play is.

Resource: The first part of the Ancient Greece scene,
up to the line "And so the play began". Story books
in school. Books about ancient Greece and its myths.
The Kenneth's Home scene. Other books in school
related to play. A trip to a theater or visit to school
of a theater company.

Context: The world of ancient Greece and its myths.
The world of drama in various media—theater,
television, video, film.

Programme of Study: Pupils can be helped to listen and
respond, and to take an interest in words and their

meanings. Pupils learn to tell and enact stories,
to participate in drama activities, including
improvisation and role-play, and to perform to an
audience. They extend and enrich their vocabulary,
have the opportunity for independent and shared
reading of a playscript, respond imaginatively to text,
and discuss features of a play such as character, setting,
plot. They write a scene of their own.

Learning Activities: Pupils discuss the Greek story
and write/draw their own response to it. They can
improvise a situation in which one of their parents/
carers comes to their bedroom early one morning to
take them on a memorable trip. Pupils read, perform
and discuss Kenneth's Home scene. Using it as a
starting point, they improvise their own scenes of
family life. They decide their own-plot and setting
and involve role-play. They perform to each other
and to other classes.

Differentiation Opportunities: Extension work could
involve reading the Ancient Greece scene, writing a
review of it and/or Kenneth's Home scene, and writing
out their improvised scene. Those with learning
difficulties could undertake listening activities based
on the sounds in the scenes (e.g. the noise of the father's
footsteps or the cheering of the family watching the
television) and discuss family life.

Homework: Pupils can ask their parents/carers about
memorable trips they made as children; they can talk
about family life in preparation for creating their own
scenes.

Learning Outcomes: Pupils begin to recognise the
features of a story and to develop listening skills.
Pupils gain confidence in understanding what a play
is and develop skills in writing, self-expression and
communication.

Assessment: The activity can be linked to Attainment Target 1 (Speaking and Listening) and to the oral skills assessed in the end of Key Stage Standard Assessment Test in English.

Ages 12-14 (Key Stage 3; Junior High School)

Activity: Introduction to Shakespeare.

Resource: Three scenes from KENNETH'S FIRST PLAY (*Romeo and Juliet, Henry V*, Shakespeare's Day); Act 1 Scene V of *Romeo and Juliet*; Act III Scene I of *Henry V*; other Shakespeare-related resources in your school; trip to local theater.

Context: The plays of Shakespeare and his contemporaries; theater-going in Shakespeare's time.

Program of Study: Pupils can learn to listen attentively, can participate in drama activities, including role-play, and can respond to drama. They can extend their understanding of drama, extract meaning beyond the literal, analyse and discuss alternative interpretations, and consider linguistic features such as rhetoric. Pupils can write a scene of a playscript.

Learning Activities: Pupils can speak, listen to, and discuss the "Shakespeare's Day" story. They can read KENNETH'S FIRST PLAY. They can act out the *Henry V* scene and discuss Shakespeare's use of language and the implications of Kenneth's reaction. They can act out the *Romeo and Juliet* scene, improvising the situations of Kenneth and his sister's boyfriend, and discuss the scene. They can write out their own *Romeo and Juliet* scene. They can apply this technique to a moment in the Shakespeare play they are studying, or, if the set text is *Romeo and Juliet*, another Shakespeare play.

Differentiation Opportunities: Extension work can explore more of the Shakespeare play(s) beyond the moments

that are the focus for the class. The language used
by Kenneth can facilitate appreciation by pupils with
learning difficulties.

Homework: Pupils can write about the first time they
met a friend and write commentaries on the extracts
from *Romeo and Juliet* and/or *Henry V* (the speech in
full).

Learning Outcomes: KENNETH'S FIRST PLAY gives
pupils confidence in approaching a Shakespeare text
and helps them to comment meaningfully on the text.

Assessment: The activity can be linked to Attainment
Targets 1 (Speaking and Listening) and 3 (Writing)
and to the oral and writing skills assessed in the end
of Key Stage Standard Assessment Test in English.

Ages 15-16 (Key Stage 4; High School)

Activity: Analysing a play and how it works, and
developing oral skills.

Resource: KENNETH'S FIRST PLAY. Other plays being
studied, a Shakespeare, a modern text. Other resources
in school related to plays. A trip to a theater.

Context: The set plays. Drama in theater, on television,
film and video.

Program of Study: Pupils learn to listen attentively
in situations where they remain mostly silent. They
participate in drama activity, including role-play,
respond to drama, and perform an unscripted play.
They extend their understanding of drama in
performance and the variety in setting and structure.
They analyse, engage with and discuss ideas, themes
and language in drama. They analyse dramatic
techniques such as the portrayal of setting and period,

time shift and imagery. They write a playscript and develop their ability to write dialogue.

Learning Activities: Pupils can read KENNETH'S FIRST PLAY. They can perform the Ancient Greece scene, listen to it, and analyse it. They can perform the sequence of scenes Pretend/Playground/Kenneth's Home/After the Match/Moscow and analyse it in relation to role-play, character, setting, period and imagery. They can discuss the ideas and themes (e.g. attitudes to parents and siblings, the generation gap). They can use the sections in Kenneth's house as a starting point for improvising in small groups their own play about family life, which they can later script and act out to each other.

Differentiation Opportunities: Extension work can involve the study of the whole play and other plays on the syllabus. The Pretend scene can be used to facilitate analysis and discussion for those with learning difficulties.

Homework: Write a playscript based on the improvisation in class. Write about a play, T V programme, film or video that depicts a lack of understanding between children and adults.

Learning Outcomes: KENNETH'S FIRST PLAY gives pupils confidence in appreciating the world of plays and develops skills of listening, writing, self-expression and communication.

Assessment: The activity can be linked to the oral and writing skills required for examination in English Language, English Literature and Drama.

APPENDIX 1

Suggested changes in order to perform KATIE'S FIRST
PLAY

Actor 2 is male

In the *Romeo and Juliet* scene:

my sister becomes my brother; she/she's/her becomes
he/he's/his/him; boy/boyfriend becomes
girl/girlfriend; Kenneth becomes Katie; Ruth becomes
Robert; George becomes Georgina
alter stage directions as appropriate

In the Ancient Greece scene:

son becomes child

In the scene in Kenneth's Home and After the Match:

Actor 1 plays Robert, Katie's brother
Actor 2 plays Georgina, Robert's boyfriend

textual changes as in the *Romeo and Juliet* scene

the line: What color do you like? Black or purple? is
taken by Actor 2 as Georgina, turning to Robert.

In the Epilogue:

textual changes as in the *Romeo and Juliet* scene

APPENDIX 2

Suggested changes in order to perform the play in North America.

crisps becomes potato chips/ crisp packet becomes bag of chips
foyer becomes lobby
toilet becomes bathroom

In the *Henry V* scene:

Actor 1: Kenneth, we're in England now, during World War II and the whole country is under attack. Bombs are dropping. Sirens scream.

Actor 5: your country becomes England

Actor 1: delete a place called

In the Pretend scene:

delete drop

In the Playground scene:

The children pretend to play basketball

Change the teams involved in the big match as appropriate, the names of the players, and the description of what happens in the game (and continue

these changes through to the scene in Kenneth's Home).
The penalty becomes a foul shot.

In the scenes Kenneth's Home and After the Match:

sofa becomes couch
delete up
cuppa tea becomes cup of coffee
football becomes basketball
promising becomes good
Coronation Street becomes *Guiding Light*
mum becomes mom
penalty shoot out becomes overtime
at the end of the basketball game a horn could be
sounded if possible

In the After the Match scene:

changing room becomes locker room
toilet becomes bathroom
hoovering becomes vacuuming
the washing up in the kitchen becomes doing the dishes

In the Moscow scene:

pocket money becomes allowance

In the Epilogue:

crisps become potato chips
Salt and Vinegar becomes Cheddar Cheese